TOGETHER WE PRAY

Prayers and Services for Gatherings and Groups

TOGETHER WE PRAY

Carmen L. Caltagirone

ave maria press AMP Notre Dame, Indiana

www.avemariapress.com

International Standard Book Number: 1-59471-040-6

Cover and text design by Brian C. Conley

Cover illustration © 2005 Emese Rivera

Printed and bound in the United States of America.

Library of Congress Cataloging-in-Publication Data
Caltagirone, Carmen L.
    Together we pray : prayers and services for gatherings and
groups / Carmen L. Caltagirone.
        p. cm.
    Includes bibliographical references.
    ISBN 1-59471-040-6 (pbk.)
    1. Worship programs. 2. Prayers.   I. Title.
BV198.C35 2005
264'.13--dc22

                                                              2004026805

These prayers are dedicated to
Colleen K. Brady,
who, while I wrote them, was truly
"the wind beneath my wings"
and
to the memory of
Gennaro Louis La Manna

CONTENTS

INTRODUCTION

We convene gatherings to make major as well as incidental decisions, to plan, assess, and solve problems. We gather to celebrate unity, rejoice in certain milestones, and recognize various accomplishments. These prayers are intended to enhance such gatherings and acknowledge God's role in them and in all of life. Because they resonate with human experiences, a community struggling with change, grief or discord should be able to identify with the sentiment in certain of these prayers and so connect with God. Other groups who are rejoicing, beginning projects or celebrating recent accomplishments will readily identify with others.

The sentiments expressed in these prayers come from places I have been in my own spiritual journey and especially from the people I have met along the way. They have shared their stories and their heart's yearnings with me. I have always been very introspective and an attentive observer of human life. Many of these prayers come from what I have seen and heard and felt by watching the unfolding drama of human life. These prayers have welled up inside me from seeing the anguish of parents at the burial site of their child and the joy of a wife on the day of her husband's return from war. These prayers flowed from seeing the pain and emptiness in the eyes of a nursing home resident and the tenderness of a father holding his special-needs daughter in his arms. Seeing the innocence, radiance, and hope in the smiles of children every day has called forth many of these prayers from deep inside of me.

These prayers also came from my own personal joy and brokenness. I have lived many of these prayers. I have shouted them, cried them, or whispered them in the dark. As I grow older and as I meet new and sometimes unimaginable challenges in my ministry, I find myself praying more and more. The real life, lived experience of soul-wrenching prayer is the undercurrent of the prayers in this collection. Lots of living went into these prayers.

I believe ministerial groups and other groups bonded by some common ground, like families, neighbors, or support groups, must look inward to God for guidance every step of the way. The prayers in this book can be a way for these groups to acknowledge that not only is God present in their gathering and their plans but at the center of all that they do.

Words are powerful; they sometimes give shape and expression to what is deep in our souls. They have the power to express our innermost yearnings. They hold secrets and sometimes hide the truth. Words can bring us laughter and they can cause great pain. Words can become hymns of joy or dirges of despair. They reach deep inside and touch the depths of our very souls. In these prayers I use ordinary words, which can often be the most powerful, with the hope that they will resonate in those who use them, drawing persons and groups closer to God.

While words are indeed wonderful tools, they alone are never enough in our human relationships or in our relationship with God. No words can fully express the essence of the soul, for that only happens in the fullness of relationship with God. I hope that beneath the maze of words and the complexities of language, those who pray these prayers will find a deep and genuine connection to the God of our desires.

We live in an extraordinary time. We live in an era of tremendous human advances, especially in communications. We carry tiny telephones in our pockets and call family and friends from the supermarket checkout line. We access millions of bits of information with the click of a mouse and squeeze all the books in our public library onto a slim, compact disk. Yet in the midst of a communication revolution where we network with hundreds of thousands of people across the globe in just one instant, the connection that matters most is our connection with God.

Prayer is an integral part of that connection and of a human life fully lived. It is not something we do apart from the rest of our living. It is something we do in the midst of it. Sometimes the living itself is our prayer. Prayer is about living. It is about silence and shouting, laughing and crying, yearning and hoping. Like life itself, prayer is about clinging and letting go, pleading and giving thanks. It is about total honesty, and about praising, celebrating, and rejoicing. Prayer is about knowing unequivocally that without God nothing makes sense.

In putting together this collection of prayers, and over a lifetime of praying, I have come to believe that each of us has a special prayer deep in our souls. Some of us will spend our lives searching for it while all the time it is there within. When we finally find our deepest prayer and speak it to God, we will find true peace.

Using This Book

The deepest expressions of our connection to God often come spontaneously at surprising moments in human experience. However, formalized, structured prayers have always held a prominent place in religious tradition. They form a framework for our faith by giving expression to our need for God. All of the prayers in this volume have some specific form to them. They provide a framework for faith and lead those who use them into deeper union with God.

Most of the prayers are written in the first person plural because they are intended for groups to pray in community. If desired, a single individual can pray each of the prayers alone. All that is required is slight modifications in the use of pronouns. The prayers can also be used for reflective reading. In whatever way they are used, these prayers are an invitation to step deeper into ourselves and discover God who dwells there.

There are two parts in this collection. The first is made up of prayer services and the second is made up of shorter prayers. The prayer services have varied structures with some typical or common elements. Usually, there are individual prayers with scripture readings and responses. Some have prayers of petition, blessings, readings from sources other than scripture, litanies, and closing prayers. Some have prayers specific to the theme of the service.

Some of the prayers in the second section, while shorter, are still divided into parts. Like the prayer services, there are usually parts for a leader and parts for everyone gathered. Other prayers in this section are simply presented as a single piece. These can be prayed aloud in unison by all gathered or divided into parts. They can also be read aloud by a single individual while others listen prayerfully, or read aloud by several individuals who take turns praying certain lines. These shorter prayers can be used in many different ways and are particularly useful for beginning or ending meetings and other simple gatherings.

In this second part, there are five categories. These include 1) Seasonal Prayers, 2) Morning Prayers, 3) Night Prayers, 4) Prayers for Meetings and 5) Prayers to Celebrate our Human Journey. All the prayers in the collection can be used as meeting prayers. However, those in the section labeled "Meeting Prayers" make reference explicitly to the dynamics of meetings. For example they refer to decision-making, listening, speaking openly and honestly, being responsible, etc.

When using this book, carefully consider the environment in which you pray and the posture that you use. I have offered some suggestions at the beginning of each of the prayer services, and here are some questions to ask in preparing to pray, especially with groups.

- Shall we sit, stand, kneel or use some combination of postures?
- How close together should we be?
- Will music enhance the setting? At what points in the

prayer should we use it?
- What should the lighting be, bright lights or dim?
- Do I need to gather any items for this prayer? (a bible, copies of prayers or responses, a cross, candle, bowl of water?)
- What should be the pace of this prayer? Where are pauses needed and how long should they be? (Customary places are at transitions between various elements, after scripture readings, and after the invitation to pray.)
- What roles need to be filled for the prayer (leader, readers, etc.)? What detailed instructions do they need? Should we rehearse anything?

I have tried throughout this book to use inclusive language. However, all quotations from Scripture and other sources appear just as they do in the copyrighted texts. In some instances, I did not choose inclusive language if it seemed awkward and broke the flow of the prayer. I find it regrettable that the English language does not have gender-neutral personal pronouns in the third person singular that can be used when referring to God.

When duplicating any of the prayers or services, be sure to follow the permissions outlined on the copyright page at the front of the book.

Acknowledgments

I believe we each are on a mystical journey we call life. Those who journey with us enrich our unique passages. I thank God daily for those who have walked the way with me. I believe there is a holy place inside each of us, a sanctuary wherein dwell all those who have touched our lives. Those who dwell there continue to bless us with their enduring presence. I want to acknowledge all whose presence has enriched my vision of life and helped me write these prayers.

I thank my parents who taught me to love. I thank the students, both past and present, at The Academy of the Holy Names where I am principal. They remind me daily that love and goodness still reign in the world. My friend, Sister Ann Regan, S.N.J.M., blesses all my days. I do not know anyone who is more alive. I am grateful for her down-to-earth wisdom and her love of life. She is not only my sounding board, but was an excellent critic in refining these prayers. Colleen K. Brady has been one of God's best surprises in my life. She fuels my enthusiasm for life and ministry, and inspires me with her vision that sees beyond seeing. Finally, Glenda Sinardi came into our family and brought a breath of fresh air. Her affirming manner is truly a blessing to me.

Rabbi Abraham Heschel once wrote "Different are the languages of prayer, but the tears are the same." I believe that prayer is mostly about yearning, and though our words and sentiments vary, what is deep in our souls is the same. It is an outrageous longing for the comfort and peace that only God can give. These prayers are really for those of you who have awakened in the middle of the night frightened because, although you live a relatively contented life, there is something unsettling within you, something that yearns and aches and cries out for more. I offer these prayers in thanksgiving to God, who continues to affirm me in so many ways.

MAY 31, 2003
FEAST OF THE VISITATION

PART I: PRAYER SERVICES

WELCOMING A NEW DAY

Consider gathering outdoors for this service. The sights, sounds, and smells will enhance this simple service.

Opening Prayer

Leader: Mindful that we are in God's presence, let us pray.

All: **Glorious God,**
the dawn has given birth to this new day.
We who waited in darkness
are overwhelmed by your magnificent light.
Aware of the beauty of this day
and the privilege of being alive and free,
we praise you for being our God.

A Song of Praise   Psalm 100:1–2, 4–5

Leader: Let us offer our praises to God.

All: **Make a joyful noise to the LORD, all the earth.**
Worship the LORD with gladness;
come into his presence with singing.
Know that the LORD is God.
It is he that made us, and we are his;
we are his people, and the sheep of his pasture.
Enter his gates with thanksgiving,
and his courts with praise.
Give thanks to him, bless his name.
For the LORD is good;
his steadfast love endures forever,
and his faithfulness to all generations.

Listening to God's Word

Leader: Let us listen attentively to the proclamation of God's saving word.

Reader: A reading from the first Letter of Paul to the
Thessalonians 5:14–22

Response Psalm

119:65–68

Side A:　You have dealt well with your servant,
O LORD, according to your word.

Side B:　Teach me good judgment and knowledge,
for I believe in your commandments.

Side A:　Before I was humbled I went astray,
but now I keep your word.

Side B:　You are good and do good;
teach me your statutes.

Prayers of Petition

Leader:　Confident of God's love for us let us offer our prayers of petition.

Leader:　Ever-present God,
awaken our hearts to your presence among us.

All:　**May we see you in every person we meet today,
in every pair of eyes, and in every hand extended.
May we see you in the smallest person we meet today,
in the most callous person,
in the neediest person,
and in all those with whom we live and work.**

Leader:　Almighty God, give us strength this day.

All:　**May we meet the crosses
that await us in the problems of this day
and the surprises hidden
in the upcoming hours
with fidelity and courage.**

Leader:　Holy God, walk with us throughout this day.

All:　**Make us holy.
Keep us tuned in
to the word you will speak to us
in the events of this day.
Keep us ever-mindful that we will do nothing today,
or any day,**

**on our own.
You are always with us**

**to guide and sustain us,
to console and hold us close in the midst of trouble.**

Blessing

Leader: May the God of goodness
journey with us through this day.
May the God of wisdom and understanding
inspire us.
May the God of tenderness and compassion
fill our hearts with holy love.
May the God of blessings
watch over all of our comings and our goings
today and every day.

All: **Amen.**

BEGINNING A DAY OF MINISTRY

This prayer service is intended for a group that has gathered to spend a day in service work or in other ministry together. Consider arranging chairs in a circle.

Opening Prayer

Leader: We give you thanks, God of light,
for sustaining us through the night
and bringing us to the light of this new day.

All: **Open our eyes to your light and our ears to your Word.**

Listening to God's Word

Leader: God will speak a word to us. Let us open our hearts and minds.

Reader: A reading from the first Letter of Peter   1:3–5

Response   Psalm 34:1–5, 8, 18, 22

Side A: I will bless the LORD at all times;
his praise shall continually be in my mouth.

Side B: My soul makes its boast in the LORD,
let the humble hear and be glad.

Side A: O magnify the LORD with me,
and let us exalt his name together.

Side B: I sought the LORD, and he answered me,
and delivered me from all my fears.

Side A: Look to him, and be radiant;
so your faces shall never be ashamed.

Side B: O taste and see that the LORD is good;
happy are those who take refuge in him.

Side A: The LORD is near to the brokenhearted,
and saves the crushed in spirit.

Side B: The LORD redeems the life of his servants;
none of those who take refuge in him will be condemned.

Prayers of Petition

Leader: Let us bring our needs before our loving God.

Leader: God of all creation,
hear our morning prayer
as we lift our hearts, minds, and souls to you.
Watch over all that we do this day.
Make our every purpose holy.

All: **May we be generous with the gift of ourselves.
May we be sincere, understanding, and loving
toward every person we meet.
God of love,
May we spend this day in intimacy with you.**

Leader: God of wisdom,
may we hear your word in the events of this day.

All: **May we respond with all our hearts to every person we
meet
and may we see in them a glimpse of you, God of love.
May we patiently embrace the crosses that we confront
today.
As we bear them, may we remember the cross
that Jesus bore for us.**

Leader: Sustainer God,
there are many who will need you in a special way today.
At this moment we lift them up to you:

The leader and other participants mention aloud the names of persons with special needs.

All: **Shower them with your love and care;
hold them close to your heart.**

Closing Prayer

All: **Wondrous God,**

let our prayers be joined
with the prayers of all those who pray today.
When this day draws to an end,
may we be able to reflect on it with holy satisfaction,
knowing that we have served you well.
Throughout this day, and every day,
we place our lives in your holy hands.
Amen.

COME, LORD JESUS (AN ADVENT PRAYER)

Advent is a time of hope-filled anticipation of the promise of salvation. Always and everywhere we pray that Christ comes to renew our lives.

Call to Worship

Leader: Something new is happening among us!
Christ comes to renew us.
Yes, Christ comes to make us new in our ministry,
in our families and communities,
and in our relationships with him.
The newness of Christ is life-giving
though it may break our routines and frighten us,
shaking us loose from our certainties.
The God of our longing comes
to disturb us from our complacency,
but he also comes with new hope
for a tomorrow filled with promise.

Leader: Let us pray.

All: **God of promises,**
we are men and women of hope.
We come before you today
announcing our enthusiasm
for your renewed coming into our lives.
We cling to your promise of life
and we await you full of hope.
Come, Lord Jesus.

Listening to God's Word

Leader: In this time and in this place God will speak to our hearts through the prophets Isaiah, Ezekiel, and Jeremiah.

Reader 1:   Do not remember the former things,
or consider the things of old.
I am about to do a new thing;
now it springs forth,
do you not perceive it?
I will make a way in the wilderness
and rivers in the desert.

Isaiah 43:18–19

All: **See, I am doing something new!**
            Now it springs forth, do you not perceive it?

Reader 2: Thus says the Lord God:
            I will gather you from the peoples,
            and assemble you out of the countries
            where you have been scattered,
            and I will give you the land of Israel.
            When they come there, they will remove from it
            all its detestable things and all its abominations.
            I will give them one heart, and put a new spirit within them;

                                              Ezekiel 11:17–19a

All: **See, I am doing something new!**
            Now it springs forth, do you not perceive it?

Reader 3: I will remove the heart of stone from their flesh
            and give them a heart of flesh,
            so that they may follow my statutes
            and keep my ordinances and obey them.
            Then they shall be my people, and I will be their God.

                                              Ezekiel 11:19b–20

All: **See, I am doing something new!**
            Now it springs forth, do you not perceive it?

Reader 4: But this is the covenant that I will make
            with the house of Israel after those days, says the Lord:
            I will put my law within them,
            and I will write it on their hearts;
            and I will be their God, and they shall be my people.

                                              Jeremiah 31:33

All: **See, I am doing something new!**
            Now it springs forth, do you not perceive it?

All pause for silent reflection.

Prayers of Petition

Leader: Let us prepare our hearts for the God of promises
and open our eyes to see Christ at work in our lives.
Wonderful God,
open our hearts and make us ready to receive your love.

All: **Open our hearts, O God.**

Leader: God of promises,
lead us to the vision of a new tomorrow
where there is no more suffering, only peace.

All: **Open our hearts, O God.**

Leader: God of hope,
renew our lives with your love.
Let your Spirit work within us to remove complacency and
despair.

All: **Open our hearts, O God.**

Leader: God of the universe,
renew the face of the earth.
Let justice and peace rain down from heaven.

All: **Open our hearts, O God.**

Leader: Guide us, encourage us, and instruct us
so that we can see with new eyes
the tremendous hope which is ours
because we believe in you.

All: **Open our hearts, O God.**

Closing Prayer

All: **God of promise,
make us ready for your coming.
Help us to find quiet moments of contemplation.
Help us to see awesome beauty in one another's eyes.
Help us to hear and respond to the cries of the poor and
the oppressed.**

Help us to breathe in the wonders of nature.
Help us to walk along that path that leads to you.
Help us to find the only truth that will save us.
Help us to serve you until that day
when we meet face to face.
Help us to grow closer to you with each passing day
and to love you.
Come, Lord Jesus!
Amen.

LIVING THE PASCHAL MYSTERY

The Paschal Mystery is part of the rhythm of Christian life. Consider dim lighting and a brightly burning candle near a cross or crucifix at the center of a circle of chairs.

Introduction

Leader: It was the darkest of days
when Jesus gave up his spirit
and surrendered himself to death.
But the darkness did not last.
When morning came on the third day,
there was marvelous light.

All: **Out of darkness came the light.
Out of night came the day.
Out of sorrow came joy.
Out of death came new life.
We speak the paschal mystery with our lives.
We live it day by day.**

Opening Prayer

Leader: Let us pray.
Loving God,
we open our hearts and minds to you.
Bring us to a deeper appreciation of the life-giving power
of your paschal mystery.
May we always experience our suffering
in light of its saving grace.

All: **Amen.**

Readings and Responses

Reader 1:   From *Walking with Loneliness* by Paula Ripple, F.S.P.A.
The test of the faithful follower of Jesus is in our belief in the paschal mystery. It is in our willingness to walk into and then through our own dying until we come to our own day of rising. It is in our willingness to hand over our broken dreams as Jesus spoke of handing over his own spirit and then, like him, to claim a new spirit present in a refashioned dream.

All:　　**Loving God,**
we walk through all of life's turmoil
with confidence
because you are a God of life and light.
You who are our paschal savior,
we trust in your tender love.
Amen.

Reader 2:　Yet it was the will of the LORD to crush him with pain.
When you make his life an offering for sin,
he shall see his offspring, and shall prolong his days;
through him the will of the LORD shall prosper.
Out of his anguish he shall see light;
he shall find satisfaction through his knowledge.
The righteous one, my servant, shall make many righteous,
and he shall bear their iniquities.
Therefore I will allot him a portion with the great,
and he shall divide the spoil with the strong;
because he poured out himself to death,
and was numbered with the transgressors;
yet he bore the sin of many,
and made intercession for the transgressors.

Isaiah 53:10–12

All:　　**God is our refuge and our strength,**
a very present help in trouble.

Psalm 46:1

Reader 3:　Jesus answered them, "The hour has come for the Son of Man to
be glorified. Very truly, I tell you, unless a grain of wheat falls into
the earth and dies, it remains just a single grain; but if it dies, it
bears much fruit.

John 12:23–24

All:　　**Make me to know your ways, O LORD;**
teach me your paths.
Lead me in your truth, and teach me,
for you are the God of my salvation;
for you I wait all day long.

Psalm 25:4–5

Reader 4:   It was now about noon, and darkness came over the whole land until three in the afternoon, while the sun's light failed; and the curtain of the temple was torn in two. Then Jesus, crying with a loud voice, said, "Father, into your hands I commend my spirit." Having said this, he breathed his last.

Luke 23:44–46

All: **The LORD is near to the brokenhearted,
and saves the crushed in spirit.**

Psalm 34:18

Reverencing the Cross

The leader or an assistant holds a cross high for all to see.

Leader: This is the sign of our salvation.
The cross represents pain, submission, and death,
and yet, it is for us a sign of victory.
Christ's death on the cross won for us eternal life.
We look to it for strength,
seeing not only pain and sorrow,
but the saving power of Jesus Christ who sets us free.

The cross is passed to each person. Each in turn makes an act of reverence such as a kiss, the sign of the cross, or a moment of silence as he or she receives the cross.

Closing Prayer

Leader: Let us pray.

All: **God of life,
we rejoice in the gift of salvation and in you, our hope.
As we endure life's suffering,
we cling to your promise of life.
Jesus is our savior who transforms death into life.
We offer this, our prayer, in his holy name.
Amen.**

UNLESS YOU BECOME LIKE LITTLE CHILDREN

This is a simple prayer service asking God to restore those childlike qualities that make us humble before the magnificence of God.

Opening Prayer

Leader: Lord Jesus,
we rejoice because you called for the little children to come to you.
Give us the gift of simplicity and humility
that we might always approach you with childlike reverence.

Listening to God's Word

Leader: Open your minds and hearts to hear God's holy word.

All stand

Reader: A reading from the gospel of Matthew   18:1–4

Response   Psalm 131

Side A: O LORD, my heart is not lifted up,
my eyes are not raised too high;

Side B: I do not occupy myself with things
too great and too marvelous for me.

Side A: But I have calmed and quieted my soul,
like a weaned child with its mother;
my soul is like the weaned child that is with me.

Side B: O Israel, hope in the LORD
from this time on and forevermore.

Prayers of Petition

Leader: Recognizing our dependence on God, let us offer our heartfelt prayers.

Leader: When we seek after riches and power,

All: **Fill us with childlike holiness, simplicity, and innocence.**

Leader: When we fail to accept others as they are,

All: **Give us a childlike spirit of hospitality.**

Leader: When we barter our integrity for some of the world's glory,

All: **Give us a childlike contentment with belonging to you.**

Leader: When guilt or shame burdens us,

All: **Remind us that you are mother and father to us; that your love is unconditional.**

Leader: When we want to be something we are not,

All: **Remind us that our true identity comes from being yours.**

Closing Prayer

Leader: God of all,
we are indeed yours.
Yet we often seem disconnected and alienated from you.
Give us back the holy simplicity of childhood
and awaken the child who dwells within.
Like a child who rests in a mother's arms,
may we find rest in you.

All: **Amen.**

DREAMING OUR DREAMS

Visionary hope is an essential characteristic in ministry. This prayer service about hope is appropriate for use in a group sharing a common ministry or mission.

Call to Worship

Leader: As God's people we are dreamers.
            We dream in faith and in hope
            knowing well that because our God is a God of promises,
            dreams do come true.

Opening Prayer

Leader: Let us pray.
            God of wonder,
            teach us to dream your dreams.
            Give us a clear vision
            to see beyond the here and now
            to the wonder of what is possible
            because you love and care for us.

All: **Amen.**

Readings and Responses

Leader: With open minds, hearts, and hands, let us listen to these words of inspiration.

Reader 1:   From *Seasons of the Heart* by Macrina Wiederkehr, O.S.B.
            I am told that there are folk who refuse to dream because their dreams have been so seemingly shattered like dreams that die at birth. And they hide their dreams in small corners of their hearts and pretend they aren't there.
            But as for me I am almost sure that in the Body of Christ that we call the Church we have the power to help each other's dreams come true. For in dark moments when light has hidden its face for a while we are the stars meant to shine for each other and we do!
            More than anything else I would like to remind you that the dreams hidden within you have the power to become a gospel. And it is as important for me to know that as it is for the sun to shine or the rain to fall or a heart to beat, because only if we

believe in the gospel that lives inside those hidden dreams in us can the strangers we walk with afford to dream.

Response

All: **God of our dreams, awaken our hearts to the dreams hidden within us. May we share our dreams with one another and help each other's dreams come true.**

Reader 2: A reading from the book of the Prophet Habakkuk   2:1–3

Response

All: **God of promises,**
you have written a vision on our hearts.
We will hold fast to the vision.
It is a sign and an affirmation of your promise of life.
You give us new hope with each passing day.
Help us cling to your promises.
In all of life's trials, may we depend on you,
our ever-faithful God.

Reader 3: A reading from the book of the Prophet Joel   3:1–5

Response

Leader: God will work wonders in the heavens and on the earth!

All: **God will work wonders in the heavens and on the earth!**

Leader: We live in a splintered world, surrounded by sadness and despair.

All: **God will work wonders in the heavens and on the earth!**

Leader: All around us there are men and women without homes, without dreams, and without hope.

All: **God will work wonders in the heavens and on the earth!**

Leader: The sick, the elderly, and the unborn cry out for help.

All: **God will work wonders in the heavens and on the earth!**

Leader: Our hearts ache with the pain of all of humanity.

All: **God will work wonders in the heavens and on the earth!**

Leader: Everywhere there are broken dreams and broken promises.

All: **God will work wonders in the heavens and on the earth!**

Leader: We search but cannot always find peace.

All: **God will work wonders in the heavens and on the earth!**

Leader: We call on God to sustain us as we dream.
Faithful God, give us new vision

All: **to see beyond the routine and familiar
to the joy and peace that only you can give.**

Leader: Give us faith

All: **that we may cling to what is real.**

Leader: Give us your healing touch

All: **that we may mend our broken world.**

Leader: Give us your peace

All: **and let it reign in our world, in our homes
and especially in our hearts.**

Closing Prayer

Leader: Faithful God,
we dream because you have given us vision, faith, hope,
and security.
Without you, our dreams are worthless and our hopes empty.
Sustain us with your love as we dream and struggle.
We are men and women of faith, depending totally on you.
Dream our dreams with us
and make our dreams come true.

All: **Amen.**

IF GOD DOES NOT BUILD *(FOR BEGINNING A NEW PROJECT)*

This service can be used as a way of asking God to sanctify the efforts of a group about to begin a new project. A symbol of the new project can be prominently displayed in the prayer space.

Call to Worship

Leader: Let us come before the God of all creation with open hands and open hearts.

All: **Let us praise and thank God with every fiber of our beings.**

Leader: Our God is a God of life, full of tenderness and compassion.

All: **God calls us to build, to risk and to renew.**

Leader: God has brought us to this moment.

All: **It is a time to pause and reflect on who we are and where we are going.**

All pause in silent reflection

Remembering Our Purpose

The speakers should be positioned so that they are scattered around the room, each standing at his or her place to read.

Leader: We gather as one community of believers to reflect and to resolve.

Speaker A: We gather because we stand on the shoulders of giants.
We know our roots and celebrate our heritage.
We rejoice in having been chosen to speak God's word to God's holy people.

Speaker B: We gather because we are men and women of faith joined together in hope.
God has called us to build and to renew.
We come to forge a new tomorrow
for ourselves and those who will come after us.

Speaker C: We gather with mixed emotions,
with great anticipation, curiosity, and even some fear.
We ask God to walk with us, through this
and all the changes of our lives
and to remain with us while we plant and while we sow.

All: **Hear us, O God as we unite ourselves to you.
Give us your courage and your strength
to remain faithful to what lies ahead.**

Proclamation of the Word

Reading I

Leader: God will speak to us in this time and in this place.
Let us listen with all of our hearts.

Reader 1: A reading from the book of the Prophet Jeremiah   1:4–10

Now the word of the LORD came to me saying,

Reader 2: "Before I formed you in the womb I knew you,
and before you were born I consecrated you,
I appointed you a prophet to the nations."

Reader 1: "Ah, Lord God, truly I do not know how to speak,
for I am only a boy."

Reader 2: "Do not say, 'I am only a boy';
for you shall go to all to whom I send you,
and you shall speak whatever I command you.
Do not be afraid of them,
for I am with you to deliver you, says the LORD."

Reader 1: Then the LORD put out his hand and touched my mouth.

Reader 2: "Now I have put my words in your mouth.
See, today I appoint you over nations and over kingdoms,
to pluck up and to pull down,
to destroy and to overthrow,
to build and to plant."

Leader: This is indeed the word of God.

All: **Thanks be to God.**

Reading II

Reader 3: From the book of the Prophet Isaiah   43:1–2, 5, 10, 18–19
Do not fear, for I have redeemed you;
I have called you by name, you are mine.

Reader 4: When you pass through the waters, I will be with you;
when you walk through fire you shall not be burned.

Reader 3: Do not fear, for I am with you;
I will bring your offspring from the east,
and from the west I will gather you.

Reader 4: You are my witnesses, says the LORD,
and my servant whom I have chosen,
so that you may know and believe me.

Reader 3: Do not remember the former things,
or consider the things of old.
I am about to do a new thing;
now it springs forth, do you not perceive it?

Leader: Let us give thanks for God's holy word.

All: **All praise and thanksgiving to God**
who speaks the word of life!

The Gospel

Leader: Let us be still,

All: **for we are in the presence of God.**

Leader: Let us listen to the Good News of Jesus Christ.

All: **May we receive it in our hearts.**

Reader 5: A reading from the gospel of John   15:4–8

Response   Psalm 127:1–2

Reader 6:   Unless the LORD builds the house,
those who build it labor in vain.
Unless the LORD guards the city,
the guard keeps watch in vain.

All: **Apart from God, we can do nothing.**

Reader 5:   It is in vain that you rise up early
and go late to rest,
eating the bread of anxious toil;
for he gives sleep to his beloved.

All: **Apart from God, we can do nothing.**

Prayers of Petition

Leader: Gracious God,
through all time you listen to the pleas of your people.
You listen to the gentle prayers of children
and hear the anguished cries of those in pain.
You give ear to all who need your help.
Confident of your mercy, we present our needs to you.

Leader: When fear and uncertainty creep into our lives

All: **remind us of your protective care.**

Leader: When we are weary and reach our limits

All: **comfort and soothe us with your love.**

Leader: As we struggle to understand the meaning and purpose of change

All: **give us open minds and the gift of wisdom.**

Leader: As we grow older and confront new challenges

All: **give us the courage to meet whatever tomorrow brings.**

Leader: As we serve you

All: **help us not to count the cost.**

Leader: When our spirits dampen and enthusiasm grows dim

All: **keep us faithful to you.**

Leader: Life-giving God,
you complete all we do and are.
We are totally dependent on you.
Forgive us for ever thinking that we are self-sufficient;
for not keeping you at the center of our plans and projects.
We know that unless we allow you to work in our lives,
what we do means nothing.
God of life,
sustain us with your nurturing love.
We offer you our petitions with total confidence,
knowing that you are rich in love and mercy.

All: **Amen.**

Closing Prayer

All: **Creator God,
give us fortitude to endure change,
courage to step into tomorrow unafraid,
wisdom to make good decisions,
love and zeal to serve your people well,
and insight to recognize that apart from you
we can do nothing.
Life-giving God,
sustain us as we attempt to build and grow.
Help us meet changes with confidence,
knowing that your call comes
with the promise of fidelity.
Keep us faithful, reminding us always that
whatever we do,
we do in you, with you and through you.
We thank you, faithful God,
for your loving, constant care.
Amen.**

GOD'S GOOD EARTH

This prayer service celebrates the earth and its Creator and is intended to be celebrated outdoors. When that is not possible, consider bringing some of the outdoors in. For example, flowering branches, autumn leaves, or beautiful stones might be used to decorate the prayer environment.

Opening Prayer

Leader: God of all creation, nurturer of all things,
bless us as we gather to celebrate your good earth.
Quiet us as we become more keenly aware of that life-giving energy that you have placed within us.

All: **Send us your spirit, who is the energy
that flows within us and among us.
May the Spirit arouse us and enlighten us
to be good stewards of the earth,
the place where the Spirit moves us.
Amen.**

Listening to God's Word

This reading is proclaimed in three parts. You may want to divide the entire group into three parts or assign three smaller clusters of readers.

Leader: We listen now to the story of creation as written in the Book of Genesis.

Group A: In the beginning when God created the heavens and the earth, the earth was a formless void and darkness covered the face of the deep,
while a wind from God swept over the face of the waters.

Group B: Then God said, "Let there be light"; and there was light.

Group C: And God saw that the light was good;
and God separated the light from the darkness.
God called the light Day, and the darkness he called Night.

Group A: And there was evening and there was morning, the first day.

Group B: And God said,

"Let there be a dome in the midst of the waters,
and let it separate the waters from the waters."

Group C: God called the dome Sky.

Group A: And there was evening and there was morning, the second day.

Group B: And God said,
"Let the waters under the sky be gathered together into one place,
and let the dry land appear."

Group C: God called the dry land Earth,
and the waters that were gathered together he called seas.

Group A: And God saw that it was good.
Then God said, "Let the earth put forth vegetation:
plants yielding seed, and fruit trees of every kind on earth
that bear fruit with the seed in it."

Group B: And it was so. The earth brought forth vegetation:
plants yielding seed of every kind,
and trees of every kind bearing fruit with the seed in it.

Group C: And God saw that it was good.
And there was evening and there was morning, the third day.

Group A: And God said,
"Let there be lights in the dome of the sky
to separate the day from the night."

Group B: And it was so. God made the two great lights—
the greater light to rule the day
and the lesser light to rule the night—
and the stars.

Group C: And God saw that it was good.
And there was evening and there was morning, the fourth day.

Group A: And God said,
"Let the waters bring forth swarms of living creatures,
and let birds fly above the earth across the dome of the sky."

Group B: So God created the great sea monsters
and every living creature that moves,

of every kind,
with which the waters swarm,
and every winged bird of every kind.

Group C: And God saw that it was good.
God blessed them, saying,
"Be fruitful and multiply and fill the waters in the seas,
and let birds multiply on the earth."
And there was evening and there was morning, the fifth day.

Group A: And God said,
"Let the earth bring forth living creatures of every kind:
cattle and creeping things
and wild animals of the earth of every kind."

Group B: And it was so. God made the wild animals of the earth of every
kind,
and the cattle of every kind,
and everything that creeps upon the ground of every kind.

Group C: And God saw that it was good.

Group A: Then God said,
"Let us make humankind in our image, according to our likeness;
and let them have dominion over the fish of the sea,
and over the birds of the air, and over the cattle,
and over all the wild animals of the earth,
and over every creeping thing that creeps upon the earth."

Group B: So God created humankind in his image,
in the image of God he created them;
male and female he created them.

Group C: God blessed them, and God said to them,
"Be fruitful and multiply,
and fill the earth and subdue it;
and have dominion over the fish of the sea
and over the birds of the air
and over every living thing that moves upon the earth."

Group A: God said,
"See, I have given you every plant yielding seed
that is upon the face of all the earth,
and every tree with seed in its fruit;
you shall have them for food.

And to every beast of the earth,
and to every bird of the air,
and to everything that creeps on the earth,
everything that has the breath of life,
I have given every green plant for food."

Group B: And it was so.
God saw everything that he had made,
and indeed, it was very good.
And there was evening and there was morning, the sixth day.

Group C: Thus the heavens and the earth were finished,
and all their multitude.
And on the seventh day
God finished the work that he had done,
and he rested.

Genesis 1:1–6, 8–14, 16–31; 2:1–2

Response

Leader: God of All Creation,
We find joy in the cool, rippling stream
and see your gentleness in the billowing clouds.
We feel your steadfast love in the refreshing rain
and know your peace in the gold and red of sunset.

All: **We praise you, O God, in all your creation.**

Leader: Your majesty is evident in the wild deer and soaring eagle.
We see your greatness in the ocean
and your persistence in the morning dew.

All: **We praise you, O God, in all your creation.**

Leader: Wherever we turn, we see glimpses of your power and your peace.
We know you in towering mountains and roaring wind.
And we revel in your beauty
in blooming trees and snow-covered wood.

All: **We praise you, O God, in all your creation.**

Leader: You are with us in the bite of winter

and the promise of spring.
You are present in the ease of summer
and in autumn's golden harvest.
You are God of the earth, and we praise you.

All: **We praise you, O God, in all your creation.**

Prayer of Forgiveness

Leader: God of all creation,
you created all things for our use and enjoyment.
Sometimes through our greed and neglect,
we misuse your wonderful gifts.

All: **In all humility
and before the radiance of sun and moon,
the magnificence of birds and fish and all living things,
we ask you, O God, for contrite hearts.
Forgive us our carelessness and neglect,
our greed and blindness.
Give us gracious hearts
and renew our appreciation
for the beauty and bounty of the earth.**

A Community Blessing of the Earth

All are invited to extend their hands in blessing.

Leader: God of all creation,
we call down your blessing upon our earth.

All: **Preserve it with your tender care.
Protect it from all forms of destruction,
especially that which is caused by human hands.
Bless every seashore, every river, and every stream.
May their flow be pure and fresh.
Bless every living thing —
fish and fowl, animal and plant.
Bless the soil that yields our food
and makes our harvests rich.
Bless every mountain and valley,
every inch of sky and earth.
Bless us too, making us good caretakers of the earth.**

Keep us from neglecting its needs
and from abusing its resources.
Keep us ever mindful that the earth is your gift to us
and a precious gift indeed.
May our children for many generations to come
enjoy all the riches and beauty of the earth.
Bountiful God,
bless this good earth with fruitfulness and prosperity.
May all people dwell on this earth in peace
until that day when you call us to our eternal home
where we shall live forever with you.
Amen.

LOVE WILL KEEP US *(THE GIFT OF FRIENDSHIP)*

This prayer service should truly be a celebration. It celebrates the joys of friendships and the God who is revealed through them. Gather the group in a circle.

Opening Prayer

Leader:	Compassionate God, we learn to love from your divine heart, source of all genuine love. We praise you for sending us friends who are sacraments of that love. As we journey through life, searching and hoping, keep us mindful that Love alone sustains us.
All:	**Amen.**

Listening to God's Word

Leader:	We come to be filled with God's word. Let us listen attentively.
Reader:	A reading from the first letter of John 4:7–2

Response

All:	**Faithful friends are a sturdy shelter; whoever finds one has found a treasure. Faithful friends are beyond price; no amount can balance their worth. Faithful friends are life-saving medicine; and those who fear the Lord will find them.**

Sirach 6:14–16

Prayer of Petition

Leader:	Let us call to mind all those people whose friendship and love have been signs of God's sustaining presence. We recall them first in the silence of our hearts asking God to guide, protect, and strengthen them.

All spend several moments in silent recollection.

Leader: Now we remember these friends by naming them aloud.
           An informal litany of names begins.

Closing Prayer

Leader: Let us pray.

All: **Gracious God,**
           thank you for revealing yourself to us
           through our friendships.
           You support and affirm us
           through the warmth of other human beings.
           We find you in a friend's loving look
           and tender embrace.
           We find you in shared soul-searching
           and moments of deep connection.
           Thank you for being a God of love
           whose incarnate love sustains us.
           Help us to be good friends,
           to be selfless and freeing,
           honest and real,
           open and faithful.
           Amen.

RETURNING TO GOD (A CELEBRATION OF RECONCILIATION)

This is a celebration of reconciliation. It can be used with a large or small group as a way of spiritually returning to God's grace.

Opening Prayer

Leader: Tender God,
we come before you aware of your mercy and compassion.
May our gathering be a return to you
as we enter anew into your gracious love.

All: **We are sinners and have failed to heed your call to love.**
We have turned from you, seeking our own way,
but we have come home, sinful
and in need of your forgiveness.
We have come home to you, gracious God
because our hearts know your loving kindness.
We have come home to you
to ask forgiveness and seek comfort.
Hear our prayers and have mercy.
Amen.

Listening to the Word

Leader: Let us allow God's word to touch our very souls.

Reader: A reading from the book of the Prophet Hosea   6:1–3

Response   Psalm 32:1–7, 11

Side A: Happy are those whose transgression is forgiven,
whose sin is covered.

Side B: Happy are those to whom the LORD imputes no iniquity,
in whose spirit there is no deceit.

Side A: While I kept silence, my body wasted away
through my groaning all day long.
For day and night your hand was heavy upon me;

Side B: my strength was dried up as by the summer's heat.
Then I acknowledged my sin to you,

and I did not hide my iniquity;

Side A: I said, "I will confess my transgressions to the LORD,"
and you forgave the guilt of my sin.

Side B: Therefore let all who are faithful offer prayer to you;

Side A: at a time of distress, the rush of mighty waters
shall not reach them.

Side B: You are a hiding place for me;
you preserve me from trouble;
you surround me with glad cries of deliverance.

Side A: Be glad in the LORD and rejoice, O righteous,
and shout for joy, all you upright in heart.

Gospel

Reader: A reading from the Gospel of Luke   15:11–32

Litany of Forgiveness

Leader: Compassionate God,
with total trust in your mercy and love,
we admit our sin and ask for your healing forgiveness.

Reader: For our selfishness

All: **forgive us, loving God.**

Reader: For our arrogance

All: **forgive us, loving God.**

Reader: For our lack of humility

All: **forgive us, loving God.**

Reader: For our greed

All: **forgive us, loving God.**

Proclamation of Praise

All: **You are great indeed, God of love and mercy!**
In you and through you we are healed.
By sending Jesus to redeem us
you looked on us with boundless love,
and despite our sinfulness, gave us eternal life.
We praise and adore you for being our God,
a God of endless possibilities whose love enlivens us.
We praise and adore you for the gift of Jesus,
who frees us from all that oppresses and shatters.
We praise and adore you for the gift of life
and the gift of others with whom we share it.
We praise and adore you
for extending your forgiveness to us again and again,
for healing our hurts,
and for welcoming us back
into the warmth of your embrace.
We praise and adore you for being our God,
full of tenderness and compassion.
May our hearts never cease praising you
and may our lips always proclaim your love.

Closing Prayer

Leader: God of mercy,
you forgive all our sins.
Though we wander far from you,
you call us back into your open arms.
We rest securely there,
knowing your tenderness and compassion.
Hear our plea for forgiveness.
We make it in the name of your Son and our life, Jesus Christ.

All: **Amen.**

REMEMBERING WHO WE ARE

This prayer service is a call to remember who we are and how we came to be who we are. While intended for use in a retreat setting or on a day of reflection, it can be adapted to other settings as well.

Call to Worship

> *Leader:* God has called us to this place as one people
> to lift our hearts and minds and voices in prayer.
> Let us set aside our cares and be still.

Pause for silent meditation.

> Let us shed all those things that burden us;
> all those things that weigh us down.
> Let us quiet our souls and tune out all the world's distractions.

Pause for silent meditation.

> Let us listen attentively to God who will speak to us.

Pause for silent meditation.

> Let us enter deeply into the heart of God.

Pause for silent meditation.

Opening Prayer

> *All:* **God of all creation,**
> **we come before you in love and in peace,**
> **because we trust in your tender love.**
> **Remind us who we are.**
> **Help us remember all those people, places,**
> **and experiences**
> **that have shaped our lives and our identity.**
> **Teach us to truly remember that it is in you**
> **that we live and move and have our being.**
> **Amen.**

Litany of Remembering

Leader: It is good to pause and remember.

All: **In remembering, we are made whole again.**

Leader: So, we gather in the name of Jesus Christ

All: **to remember who we are and how we came to be
             the people we are.**

Leader: We come in gratitude

All: **to thank God for the gift of roots and especially for
             being rooted in holy, divine love.**

Leader: We come with vision

All: **to face the future unafraid,
             remembering our steadfast, faithful God.**

Leader: We come in single-heartedness

All: **knowing well that only in our saving, loving God do we
             find peace.**

Listening to God's Word

Leader: Let us open our hearts and minds to hear and receive God's holy
             word.

Reader: A reading from the Gospel of John   15:1–8

Response

All: **Life-giving vine,
             Without you, we have no identity;
             Our lives are meaningless, apart from you.
             Keep us connected to you.
             Let our souls be channels of your love and grace.
             Flow in us and through us.**

Members of the Vine

Leader: In your presence, loving God, we call to mind those who have forged the way to holiness for us by remaining true to the vine. We remember Adam and Eve, in whom you breathed the first spark of human life.

All: **May we always cherish and respect the gift of human life, a gift that only you can give.**

Leader: We remember Abraham and Sarah, who are models of faith and courage for us.

All: **May we, like them, cling to your promises and go wherever you call us.**

Leader: We remember Job, who taught us the lesson of patient endurance.

All: **May we always accept your plans for us with patience and trust.**

Leader: We remember John the Baptist, your bold and faithful herald.

All: **May we be bold in proclaiming the Good News of Jesus Christ to everyone we meet.**

Leader: We remember Mary, our Mother, who dared to say yes to intimacy with you.

All: **May we, too, speak a resounding "yes" to the call of Christian discipleship.**

Leader: We remember Peter, who was transformed by Jesus' love.

All: **May we, too, be transformed in you.**

Leader: We remember Mary Magdalen, first to announce the triumph of the resurrection.

All: **May all we say and do proclaim to the world that Jesus lives and is with us.**

Leader: We remember our own parents and friends, who have helped form our hearts to serve you.

All: **May we always see them as sacraments of your love.**

Leader: Today and every day we remember Jesus, our Brother and our Savior. We remember his peace and his joy and especially his abiding love, a love deeper and richer than the world has ever known.

All: **May we recognize Jesus' love in our hearts. May we generously allow that love to overflow into the hearts of everyone we meet.**

Closing Prayer

Leader: Loving God,
your outrageous love for us is mirrored
in men and women of faith,
men and women who struggled with hard decisions,
men and women who belong to you.
We are rooted in them—
in Adam and Eve, Abraham and Sarah,
Job, John, Mary, Peter and Mary Magdalen.
We are rooted in those particular persons
you have sent into our lives.
Above all, we are rooted in Jesus Christ!
In him we live and move and have our being.

All: **Loving God,
we praise you for being a life-giving vine.
Keep us close to you
and never let us be separated from you.
Amen.**

TRUE RICHES

This is a celebration of all the things in life that really matter. It is especially a celebration of our identity as the people of God. It is a celebration of riches, not the riches of the world, but the spiritual riches involved with being a people connected to God.

Introduction

Leader: We live in a world that often judges us, not by the spirit within, but by the ability to earn, own, and consume. Sometimes the size of one's heart seems not as important as the size of one's bank account. We live in a world wounded by confused priorities and blind greed.

Opening Prayer

All: **God of mercy and love,
we come before you, asking you to take all our desires
and aspirations for things that do not matter
and transform them into a zealous desire
for the gifts of your Spirit.
We make our prayer through that same Spirit.
Amen.**

Listening to God's Word

Leader: God of all people,
let your word in all its richness
sink to the very center of our souls.
May it transform our lives
so that we will only seek after that which endures forever.

Reader 1:   And he said to them, "Take care! Be on your guard against all kinds of greed;
for one's life does not consist in the abundance of possessions."

Luke 12:15

All: **Loving God,
remind us that we are rich, not because we have money,
but because we have your life within us.**

Reader 2: "Do not store up for yourselves treasures on earth, where moth and rust consume and where thieves break in and steal."

Matthew 6:19

All: **Loving God,**
guide us away from greed
and help us to concentrate on you
and your graciousness.

Reader 3: Keep your lives free from the love of money, and be content with what you have; for he has said, "I will never leave you or forsake you." So we can say with confidence, "The Lord is my helper; I will not be afraid. What can anyone do to me?"

Hebrews 13:5–6

All: **Loving God,**
only in you will we know true peace.
There are no earthly riches that will satisfy us
as will the peace that only you can give.

Reader 4: Then he told them a parable:
"The land of a rich man produced abundantly.
And he thought to himself, 'What should I do,
for I have no place to store my crops?'
Then he said, 'I will do this: I will pull down my barns
and build larger ones, and there I will store all my grain and my goods.
And I will say to my soul, "Soul, you have ample goods
laid up for many years; relax, eat, drink, be merry."'
But God said to him, 'You fool!
This very night your life is being demanded of you.
And the things you have prepared, whose will they be?'
So it is with those who store up treasures for themselves
but are not rich toward God."

Luke 12:16–21

Psalm Reading

115:1–4, 9–18

Side A: Not to us, O Lord, not to us, but to your name give glory,
for the sake of your steadfast love and your faithfulness.

Side B: Why should the nations say,
"Where is their God?"

Our God is in the heavens;
he does whatever he pleases.

Side A: Their idols are silver and gold,
the work of human hands.

Side B: O Israel, trust in the LORD!
He is their help and their shield.

Side A: O house of Aaron, trust in the LORD!
He is their help and their shield.

Side B: You who fear the LORD, trust in the LORD!
He is their help and their shield.

Side A: The LORD has been mindful of us; he will bless us;

Side B: he will bless those who fear the LORD,
both small and great.

Side A: May the LORD give you increase,
both you and your children.

Side B: May you be blessed by the LORD,
who made heaven and earth.

Side A: The heavens are the LORD's heavens,
but the earth he has given to human beings.

Side B: The dead do not praise the LORD,
nor do any that go down into silence.

Side A: But we will bless the LORD
from this time and forevermore.

Prayer for Forgiveness

Leader: We come before our God, who is full of compassion,
to ask for forgiveness and mercy.

Reader: When in our excesses we consume more than our share
while others go with basic needs unmet:

All: **Forgive us, merciful God.**

Reader: When we are blinded by our affluence and fail to reach out
in care and concern:

All: **Forgive us, merciful God.**

Reader: When we are overwhelmed by desires to acquire and consume
more than we need:

All: **Forgive us, merciful God.**

Reader: When possessions cloud our view of you and your gracious love:

All: **Forgive us, merciful God.**

Closing Prayer

All: **Loving God,
we are grateful for the many blessings you bestow on us.
Help us focus on you and the blessing of life itself.
Keep us from excess.
Keep us centered in your love.
Amen.**

LIVING WATER

Water as a life-giving source is the theme throughout this prayer service. Ideally, it should be celebrated where water can be a visual focal point. The sound of flowing water will enhance the setting even further. Consider a place outdoors or around a parish baptismal font.

Call to Worship

Leader: Let us come before the God of our longings.

All: **Inhabit our hearts, wondrous God of all creation, as once you inhabited living flesh.**

Leader: Open your eyes, your hearts, your minds
and sense the good things we have from God.

All: **Blessed be God for the gift of water
which cleanses and refreshes us,
bringing us to new birth.**

Listening to God's Word

Leader: Let us be attentive as we hear the proclamation of God's holy word.

Reader   A reading from the book of the Prophet Isaiah   41:17–20

Response   Psalm 147:1–8, 12–18

Side A: Praise the LORD!
How good it is to sing praises to our God;
for he is gracious, and a song of praise is fitting.

Side B: The LORD builds up Jerusalem;
he gathers the outcasts of Israel.

Side A: He heals the brokenhearted,
and binds up their wounds.

Side B: He determines the number of the stars;
he gives to all of them their names.

Side A: Great is our LORD, and abundant in power;
his understanding is beyond measure.

Side B: The LORD lifts up the downtrodden;
he casts the wicked to the ground.
Sing to the LORD with thanksgiving;
make melody to our God on the lyre.
He covers the heavens with clouds,
prepares rain for the earth,
makes grass grow on the hills.

Side A: Praise the LORD, O Jerusalem!
Praise your God, O Zion!
For he strengthens the bars of your gates;
he blesses your children within you.

Side B: He grants peace within your borders;
he fills you with the finest of wheat.
He sends out his command to the earth;
his word runs swiftly.

Side A: He gives snow like wool;
he scatters frost like ashes.
He hurls down hail like crumbs—
who can stand before his cold?

Side B: He sends out his word, and melts them;
he makes his wind blow, and the waters flow.

Reader 2:   A reading from the Gospel according to John   4:4–14

Prayers of Petition

Leader: We bring all that we have and all that we are
before the God of Life.
We bring the desires of our hearts and ask for God's saving grace.

Reader: God our life,
there is evil in our world—hatred, bigotry, and exploitation

All: **cleanse our world with living water.**

Reader: God our life,
            when we become weary or complacent

All: **become a fountain of life within us.**

Reader: God our life,
            for the times we feel abandoned and afraid

All: **flood our souls with life-giving water.**

Reader: God our life,
            when the world is too much for us and we fall into despair

All: **be for us a river of hope.**

Leader: You, O God, are the source of all life.
            Nurture us and hold us close in your arms.

All: **Amen.**

Blessing

If water has been incorporated into the environment, the leader touches the water and continues:

Leader: God, you are the fountain of living water.
            Send down your blessing on this water and on each of us
            gathered here.
            Cleanse us of all that separates, destroys, and oppresses
            and make us living water to all who thirst for justice.

All: **Amen.**
            The leader sprinkles all gathered.

Closing Prayer

All: **God our life,**
            you quench our thirst and refresh our weary souls.
            Be a font of hope and healing for our world.
            Live in us so that we might bring
            comfort and sweet rejoicing
            into deserts of despair.

**Lead us, guide us,
and when our work on earth is through,
bring us home to the eternal rest of your heaven.
Amen.**

PRAYER AT THE COMPLETION OF A PROJECT

This prayer service is designed for use with a group just finishing a project or time of service. It is a celebration of God working in and through human hearts and hands. Some symbol of the project or service could be used as a visual focal point.

Call to Worship

Leader: As we finish our work together,
             let us bring all that we have and all that we are to our loving God.

All: **We open our hearts and minds and receive from the boundless fountain of God's love.**

Leader: Let us pray.

All: **Gracious God,
          pour out your Spirit on us
          that we may reflect with holy satisfaction
          on the good work we have done.
          Amen**

Listening to God's Word

Leader: Let us open our minds and hearts so that we may fully receive God's holy word.

Reader: A reading from the Gospel of Matthew.   11:28–30

Response

All: **Comforting God,
          we praise you for your soothing word.
          Plant its seed deep within us
          that we may always find consolation there.**

Prayer of Recollection

Leader: Let us call to mind all that has happened this day.

All spend some time in silent reflection

             Loving God,
             as we reflect on the work we have done,
             sharpen our memories so that we may embrace your many blessings.

All: **We give you thanks, O God**
for all the wondrous moments in our work,
for the knowledge, understanding, and insight
we have gained
and for all those whose lives
have touched our own this day.
For all the soul-to-soul encounters this day,
we give you thanks.

Leader: God of mercy,
after having served you, we seek your forgiveness.

All: **Forgive us our misdeeds this day:**
our unkind words and impatience,
our anger and mistrust of you and one another.
For everything we did which hurt you
whom we love above all things,
we ask forgiveness.

Leader: Gracious God,
mindful of those persons and situations we encountered today
that presented special needs,
we lift them to you.

All: **We humbly ask you to take these persons and situations**
into your protective, loving care.

Final Blessing

Leader: Let us call down God's blessings.

All: **God of wonder,**
you are our source and our sustenance.
Bless our simple and sometimes feeble efforts to serve you.
Remain with us as in all we do for the sake
of your holy name.
Remind us each day to take time for work and for play,
for labor and for rest.
Remind us especially to take time to rest in you.
We offer our prayer with absolute confidence
as a people of faith,
for we pray in the holy name of Jesus,
our Redeemer and our Brother.
Amen.

HEARTS ON FIRE

This prayer service invites participants to recognize and embrace the fire of the Holy Spirit which God freely gives to those who are open and waiting. Make fire a visual focal point of this prayer environment by using a large candle, or if gathered outdoors, perhaps a large fire.

Opening Prayer

Leader: God of glory,
we look to you alone, with total confidence.
We greet you with prayers of praise and thanksgiving
and open our hearts and minds to you
because we trust in your loving-kindness.
Enkindle our hearts with the fire of your love
and the strength of your Spirit who dwells within us.

All: **Amen.**

Readings and Responses

Significant silences should be allowed between each reading and response.

Leader: Let us receive these words of inspiration in our hearts.

Reader 1:   From the *Confessions* of St. Augustine
Too late have I loved you, O Beauty so ancient and so new, too late have I loved you! Behold you were within me, while I was outside: It was there that I sought you, and, a deformed creature, rushed headlong upon these things of beauty which you have made. You were with me, but I was not with you. They kept me far from you, those fair things which, if they were not in you, would not exist at all. You have called to me, and cried out, and have shattered my deafness. You have blazed forth with light, and have shone upon me, and you have put my blindness to flight! You have sent forth fragrance, and I have drawn in my breath, and I pant after you. I have tested you, and I hunger and thirst after you. You have touched me and I have burned for your peace.

Response

All: **God of life,
we your people seek you with burning hearts.
Reveal your face to us.**

Reader 2: A reading from the book of Exodus   3:1–14

Response   Psalm 141:1–2

All: **I call upon you, O Lord; come quickly to me;
give ear to my voice when I call to you.
Let my prayer be counted as incense before you,
and the lifting up of my hands as an evening sacrifice.**

Reader 3: A reading from the Gospel According to Luke   24:13–35

Response

All: **God of splendor,
our hearts still burn within us as we listen to your holy word.
Our hearts burn with joy and love
whenever we see your greatness and compassion.
You are our light and our life.**

Prayers of Petition

Leader: Mindful that we need God's help at every moment of our lives
and remembering that God hears our every need,
let us present our petitions.

Reader: Holy God, when we feel burdened and overwhelmed

All: **Send us your healing strength to console and comfort us.**

Reader: Holy God, at those times when we lose our zest for life,
when we become listless and lifeless

All: **Charge us with your own energy.**

Reader: Holy God, when we are confused and disturbed

All: **Renew us with your love;
calm us with the realization that you
give all things order.**

Reader: Holy God, when our hearts become dull

All: **Set them on fire again with your love.**

Reader: Holy God, if ever we should stop believing and hoping

All: **Remind us that you are a God of promises
             and that there are yet many glorious surprises
             in store for us.**

Closing Prayer

Leader: Let us pray.
             May our passionate God enkindle our hearts
             with the fire of the Holy Spirit.
             May that same Spirit give us new energy and new hope.
             May God charge our hearts with the fire of passionate love
             so that we may be for one another a sign of God's Spirit
             present in the world.

All: **Amen.**

CELEBRATING A FAITHFUL GOD

God's total fidelity is at the root of our salvation and the cause of our deepest joy. This prayer service is a joyful celebration of God's fidelity. The mood and environment should be festive.

Call to Worship

Leader: Let us raise our spirits and our voices to God in praise.

All: **Praise the LORD, all you nations!**
Extol him, all you peoples!
For great is his steadfast love toward us,
and the faithfulness of the LORD endures forever.

Psalm 117

Listening To God's Word

Leader: Come now before the God of all nations to hear the holy word.

Reader 1:   A reading from the book of the prophet Isaiah   41:9–10, 13

All: **Surely God is my salvation;**
I will trust, and will not be afraid,
for the LORD GOD is my strength and my might;
he has become my salvation.

Isaiah 12:2

Reader 2:   A reading from the Letter to the Romans   8:35–39

All: **I will sing of your steadfast love, O LORD, forever;**
with my mouth I will proclaim your faithfulness to all
generations.
I declare that your steadfast love is established forever;
your faithfulness is as firm as the heavens.

Psalm 89:1–2

Affirmation of Faith

Leader: Together let us affirm our faith in an ever-faithful God.

All: **We believe in a faithful God whose abundant love sustains us.**
We believe in a God who holds us close;
a God who gathers us as one people, one body.
We believe in a God whose love is unconditional.
We believe in the Holy Spirit of God
who inspires and uplifts us, arouses and animates us.
We believe in a persistent, unrelenting, unyielding God
who never leaves us alone.
We believe in an ever-present God
whose constant desire is to be with us,
to enter our hearts and to remain there forever.
Amen.

Prayers of Petition

Leader: Ever-faithful God,
mindful of your fidelity and your boundless love for us,
we humbly come before you to seek your help as we struggle to be
holy.

Reader: When daily trials overwhelm us

All: **help us seek refuge in your arms.**

Reader: When there seems to be nothing that is reliable and lasting

All: **remind us of your fidelity.**

Reader: When others betray us

All: **remind us of your steadfast love.**

Reader: When we lose heart and hope

All: **keep us ever faithful.**

Closing Prayer

Leader: Faithful God,
let us cling to your promise of life
and draw from it all that we need to be whole and holy.

All: **Amen.**

LONGING FOR GOD

Our longing for God is the true source of our restlessness. With these prayers, a group can acknowledge that restlessness and ask God for peace, the peace that only God can give.

Opening Prayer

Leader: God of our salvation,
We gather in the name of Jesus
to open ourselves to the power of the Spirit.
We struggle with many silent longings,
but we long for you most of all.
Come and satisfy our hungers.

All: **Amen.**

Leader: Let us join the psalmist in acknowledging our soul's yearnings.

Side A: As a deer longs for flowing streams,
so my soul longs for you, O God.

Side B: My soul thirsts for God,
for the living God.
When shall I come and behold
the face of God?

Side A: My tears have been my food
day and night,
while people say to me continually,
"Where is your God?"

Side B: These things I remember,
as I pour out my soul:
how I went with the throng,
and led them in procession to the house of God,
with glad shouts and songs of thanksgiving,
a multitude keeping festival.

Side A: Why are you cast down, O my soul,
and why are you disquieted within me?
Hope in God; for I shall again praise him,
my help and my God.

Side B: By day the Lord commands his steadfast love,
and at night his song is with me,
a prayer to the God of my life.

Psalm 42:1–6, 8

Prayers of Petition

Leader: Let us bring our petitions before the God of our longings.

Reader: Indeed, our souls long for you, the living God.

All: **Give us the peace that only you can give.**

Reader: Wondrous God, we long to see your face.

All: **Show us your beauty in the signs that surround us.**

Reader: Redeemer God, you are our hope and our salvation.

All: **Teach us to trust in you.**

Reader: God of promises, we cherish the covenant of love
you entered into with each of us
when we were first conceived in the secret of the womb.

All: **Nourish and sustain us with your promises.**

Psalm Reading

Side A: O God, you are my God, I seek you,
my soul thirsts for you;
my flesh faints for you,
as in a dry and weary land where there is no water.

Side B: So I have looked upon you in the sanctuary,
beholding your power and glory.

Side A: Because your steadfast love is better than life,
my lips will praise you.

Side B: So I will bless you as long as I live;
I will lift up my hands and call on your name.

Side A: My soul is satisfied as with a rich feast,
and my mouth praises you with joyful lips

Side B: when I think of you on my bed,
and meditate on you in the watches of the night;

Side A: for you have been my help,
and in the shadow of your wings I sing for joy.

Side B: My soul clings to you;
your right hand upholds me.

Psalm 63:1–8

Closing Prayer

All: **God of our longings,
no matter what comforts and securities
this world provides us,
we will never rest until we rest in your arms.
Take our longing hearts and hold them close to your own.
Fill our hearts with your peace.
Amen.**

WE ARE THE LIGHT OF THE WORLD

Through this prayer service those gathered celebrate themselves as the chosen of God. Burning candles should be prominent in the prayer space.

Introduction

Leader: God chose us, before we were even aware of it,
to be bearers of light.
We are God's light, shining brightly for all to see.
We are God's living word, spoken loudly and freely.
We give voice and flesh to God's compassion,
in and through our own tenderness, care, and fidelity.
Indeed, we are bearers of the love of a God who is love.

Opening Prayer

Leader: Loving God,
We rejoice in having been chosen to be the bearers of your light,
your word, your love, and your life.
We rely on you to guide us on our journey.
Send us your Holy Spirit,
the spirit of wisdom, understanding, and fortitude
to light our way.
Send us your compassion, so that as one community
we can unleash your power among us.

All: **Amen.**

Listening to God's Word

Leader: Let us assume a posture of attentive listening.

Reader: A reading of the Gospel according to Matthew   5:14–16

Prayer of Petition

Leader: Gracious God,
without your light nothing makes sense.
Send us your light and give us what we need.

Reader: Help us, good and loving God

All: **to hear your call of love above the noise of hectic lives.**

Reader: Help us, good and loving God

All: **to risk being open.**

Reader: Help us, good and loving God

All: **to live with uncertainties.**

Reader: Help us, good and loving God

All: **to listen to others and serve them well.**

Reader: Help us, good and loving God

All: **to change that which must be changed.**

Reader: Help us, good and loving God

All: **to give of ourselves without counting the cost.**

Reader: Help us, good and loving God

All: **to hold fast to our dreams and never lose hope.**

A Commitment

Leader: God knows and loves each of us
and has called us by name
to be light for the world.
Let us commit ourselves to be light,
especially in those places where there is great darkness.

All: **God has created me to serve and to love
and has committed some work to me
that was given to no one else.
I am in some way necessary for God's purposes in the world.
I am a part of God's great work.
I shall be an instrument of peace,
one who speaks the truth.**

I shall bear God's light for all to see.
I will serve God with all my heart.

Closing Prayer

All: **God of light,
there is no light apart from you.
Give us the courage and fortitude
to always embrace your light,
to live in your light and to share it
with all whom we meet.
Amen.**

Summer Sabbath

Summer is often thought of as a time of rest. This prayer service is an invitation to rest and rejuvenate while savoring the gifts of God.

Introduction

Leader: In the Judeo-Christian tradition, the idea of the Sabbath is central. The Jewish traditions in which Jesus grew up taught that the Sabbath is a time of rest and reward. The Sabbath is rooted in the seventh day of creation, when God did three things: God rested, blessed and made time holy. It was on the seventh day that God rested in the wonder of creation. This is a Sabbath time for us. It is a time to stop and savor life in the summer sun. Let us use this sacred summer time to pause and acknowledge the good things in our lives and our lavish, wondrous Creator. In the Sabbath time we care for the seed of eternity planted deep in our souls. We make time holy, letting the fertile ground of our lives lie fallow. Unless we are willing to be still, to withdraw from our busy-ness, to rest in the way Sabbath teaches us, we will lose our very selves.

Sabbath Prayer

Leader: May we be aware
of God's presence along our way,
helping us to discover
the peace and rest
some have lost
or never known,
renewing our covenant of peace
with all created things.

All: **And may we become more than we have been,**
more than we are:
reaching for a perfection beyond our grasp,
growing and learning one day
to make this day's peace a peace for all days,
learning one day to do justly,
and love mercy,
and walk alongside the One who walks with us.

(From *Gates of Prayer*, Central Conference of American Rabbis)

An Offering

Leader: There have been too many days when we have spent our time seeking, counting, measuring.
We have exhausted ourselves and have grown weary.

All: **In this Sabbath time,
we will seek not to acquire, but to share;
not to toil, but to relax and to celebrate.**

Leader: Many a day we have failed to see the wonder,
the grace, and the beauty of God's universe.

All: **In this Sabbath time, we stand in awe
before the mystery of all creation and its Creator.**

Leader: There have been countless days when we have acted as if everything depended on us.

All: **In this Sabbath time, we know deep in our souls that we can do nothing without God's presence and love to sustain us.**

In Thanksgiving

Leader: We welcome this summer Sabbath as a time of rest and renewal,
a time to re-create ourselves.
God of peace,
we come to this Sabbath
with grateful hearts.

Reader: For all the good things we have experienced with the change of each season

All: **we give you thanks.**

Reader: For sustaining us through all the dark nights

All: **we give you thanks.**

Reader: For making us partners with you in the re-creation of the world

All: **we give you thanks.**

Blessing

Leader: Let us bow our heads and ask for God's blessing.
May the quiet moments of summer give us a Sabbath spirit.
May this Sabbath strengthen us for the challenges that lie ahead.
May God, who calls us to this time of rest,
be with us in the resting and in the rejoicing.
May the blessings of the Sabbath soothe our souls and remain with us forever.

All: **Amen.**

PART II: SHORT PRAYERS

MORNING PRAYERS

A NEW BEGINNING

God of goodness,
you, indeed, are a God who is ever new.
Today is a new beginning,
a time to put aside what troubled us yesterday
and start anew.
Give us new hope and a fresh outlook,
that we may enjoy each other and our world.
We praise you for creating us, making us in your own image.
We praise you for your magnificent universe.
We thank you for that incredible gift.

Loving God,
help us to drink in every moment of this day,
to see the miracles that unfold within it;
to experience your hand in all that happens
and to catch a glimpse of you in one another's eyes.
Amen.

FIXING OUR MINDS ON GOD

Compassionate God,
for just a few moments this morning we pause to fix our minds on you.
We come with many needs.
We ask your help for all those who are in need:
for those who suffer because of illness, poverty, ignorance, or oppression,
for all those who have lost hope and suffer despair,
for those who mourn and are in need of comfort,
for all whom we love,
for those who feel no love, we pray.
Keep us connected to you throughout this day,
remembering that we belong to you
and that everything we do today should glorify your name.
Help us to make this day a holy day.
Amen.

EXPERIENCING THE DAY FULLY

God of wonder,
On the day we were born you began your work in us.
We know that you continue to work not only in us but through us.
Help us be good servants, always doing your work
with open and eager hearts.
Whatever comes our way today, keep us positive and peaceful,
always mindful of your presence and sustaining love among us.
Give us strength and courage to experience fully each moment of this day.
Heal all that is painful in us and give us your peace.
Watch over us, protect and guide us throughout this and every day.
Amen.

FILL US WITH ENERGY

God of all creation,
fill us with your energy and use us today to do your work.
Bless the work of our minds.
Bless the work of our hands.
Bless us each moment of this day with your presence.
We are willing;
we are ready.
Free us for whatever you have in store for us this day.
Give us positive attitudes, grateful hearts, and gentle spirits.
Remind us that we have the power to touch human hearts with your love.
We pray because we believe,
we trust, and we hope in you who are ever faithful.
Amen.

WE BELONG TO GOD

Gentle God,
you have created us in your own image and chosen us as your people.
We belong to you.
In our belonging we sense the love and security
that only come from you.
Be with us throughout this day,
especially during the more challenging moments.
Give us a true peace,
so that no matter what comes our way,
we will be able to face it with confidence and hope.
Amen.

GOD OUR REFUGE

God of peace,
whatever happens today, remind us that we can always take refuge in you.
There is nothing that will happen today
of which you will not be a part,
if only we invite you in.
Open our hearts and minds to your presence.
Take us and use us for the good of your people.
Stay close to us throughout this day.
Protect us from all harm and guide us in the right path,
the path that will always bring us home to you.
Sheltering God,
we dedicate ourselves to you this day.
Amen.

GIVE US TIME

Timeless God,
as we welcome the light of this new day,
allow us to drink in its fullness.
Help us to make each moment count,
and to make time for things that bring refreshment:
to see children at play;
to sit and dream
and to chat with old friends.
Help us to make time to make a difference:
to pray and to rest,
to notice and celebrate the wonder of your creation,
to look into one another's eyes,
to ask hard questions
and to wait for the answers.
Help us to make time enough not to hurry.
Fill this day with miracle moments
when life makes sense and we see clearly.
Give us moments when we embrace you alive in our lives,
when we hear good news,
when we forgive and are forgiven.
Give us moments of real honesty
and moments of deep awareness.
Let there be moments when we are moved to tears
and moments of laughter pouring out from our souls.
Let there be moments of gratitude
and moments when we behold your face.
Be with us throughout this day, gentle God.
Make the rhythm of our day keep pace with the cadence of your love.
Amen.

NIGHT PRAYERS

IN THE STILLNESS, IN THE SILENCE, IN THE DARKNESS

God of all time,
we praise you for the light and for the darkness.
In the darkness of this time,
in the stillness,
in the silence,
we turn to you.
You are our ever-present comfort.
Help us know you are here.
We pause to reflect on the events of this day:
the encounters, the crosses,
the hopes enhanced,
the dreams that crumbled and those that came true.

Pause to reflect
Loving God,
In the darkness,
in the silence,
in the stillness, of this time,
we turn to you.
Give us hearts for growth
so that we will learn from the mistakes of this day.
Allow the joys of this day to stretch us
so that we might truly celebrate life.
Amen.

CALM OUR SOULS

Ever-present God,
be with us through the hours of the night.
Be with us and calm our souls.
Whisper words of healing deep inside us
and lull us into a deep and peaceful sleep.
Awaken us tomorrow refreshed and renewed,
confident that you continue to walk with us through each new day.
Amen.

THANKSGIVING AND PETITION

Gracious God,
we thank you for the gift of this day,
for the joys and even for the sorrows.
Help us remember that it is often our sorrows that help us grow.
Continue to speak to us through the events of each day
and give us ears that hear your message.
We thank you for those people whom we encountered this day.
Continue to bless us with people who embody your love.
We thank you for the ability to love and be loved.
Continue to pour your love into our hearts each day,
for it sustains us.
Forgive us for our failure to love
for all those things we did today that caused pain
to another or to you whom we love above all things.
We praise and thank you for being the God of all people
day after day and night after night.
We praise you for being *our* God.
Be with us in the light and in the darkness.
Watch over us as we sleep.
Loving God,
we place our lives in your holy hands.
Amen.

SEASONAL PRAYERS

Advent

COME, LONG-EXPECTED SAVIOR

Come, long-expected Savior.
Arouse us with your joy.
Open our eyes to your wonder.
Whisper your peace in our heart
and send your light to all the dark corners of our lives.
Let us prepare a straight path that leads from our hearts to yours.
Come into our hearts, loving Jesus, for we feel alone and afraid.
Come into our hearts, for we are anxious and confused.
Come into our hearts, for we are broken and bewildered.
Come into our hearts, loving Jesus.
Amen.

AWAITING A NEWBORN SAVIOR

Loving God,
You sent an angel to lowly shepherds,
announcing the joyous birth of their Savior.
Announce your message of joy in us.
Let it settle deep in our hearts so that Christ is born anew there.
Send your angels to fill us with awe and wonder at his magnificent coming.
Like the shepherds, may our hearts, minds, and bodies
bring praise, honor, and glory to our glorious Savior.
Amen.

Christmastime

A CHRISTMAS BLESSING

Leader: Gentle God,
lull us into silent stillness during this season of peace and joy.
Christmas celebrations remind us
that you send fresh promises each day;
that your love, made flesh in a baby asleep in a stable,
continues to be our life-source.

All: **Help us to accept your invitation into the light
and to receive your gifts of joy and peace,
hope and wholeness.
Open us to the wonder that is you.**

Leader: Let us bow our heads for God's blessing.

May God bless us with the gift of inspiration
and create us anew each day.
May we experience each day the rush that comes
with knowing we are loved.
May we be convinced deep in our souls
that we are a source of light
to a world too often in darkness.
May God bless us with the gifts of courage and strength
to face the pain that only we can name.
May God bless us with the ability to see more clearly
not that which divides, but that which unites.
May God bless us with the gift of connecting the past
with the future
and of seeing that we are living sacraments of God's love.
May God give us compassion to touch wounded hearts
and to walk in peace with one another.
May the Christmas star be the beacon that leads us
to newfound joy and a renewed commitment to live the gospel.
May the blessings of Christ's peace be ours
as we grow and journey together in the spirit
of our common mission.
During this season of blessings,
may our hearts be cradles for the living God.

All: **Amen.**

PRAYER FOR THE NEW YEAR

Leader: As men and women of faith, we are grateful
for the regular rhythm of beginnings and endings
and the opportunity to start anew.
We begin this new year filled with hope,
recalling the words of St. Paul to the Philippians:

> *This one thing I do: forgetting what lies behind*
> *and straining forward to what lies ahead,*
> *I press on toward the goal*
> *for the prize of the heavenly call of God in Christ Jesus.*

Philippians   3:13–14

All: **Loving God,**
we face this new year with courage and conviction
to do what is necessary to enhance life,
to celebrate life, and to grow in you.

Leader: Holy God,
help us to discover the resources we have
within each one of us and together.

All: **May we use our time, our talents, and our resources wisely.**

Leader: Gracious God,
let what we see in the mirror be a source of peace to us.
May what others see in us be a source of peace to them.
Let there always be others who love us enough
to see beyond our failings.

All: **May we love others as they are**
and challenge them to be even more.
May we always be true to ourselves
and honest with one another.

Leader: God of wonder,
open to us what we have not seen or felt before.
Give us wisdom to recognize the good things you send us this year
and the patience we will need to work for them.

All: **Keep us from discouragement and disappointment, from weariness and complacency. Show us when to say "yes" and when to say "no."**

Leader: God of all time, as we move forward year after year, help us to deepen our faith and focus our vision on those things that truly matter.

All : **May we stand firm in all that grounds us in truth and holiness, going where your Spirit leads us with clear purpose and sure resolve.**

Leader: Loving God of peace, as we deliberate throughout this new year, show us those things that are important to you. Give us the grace to lay aside the things that do not work for the good of all.

All: **Multiply our faith, our dedication, and our resources and let us find new joy in serving you. Amen.**

Lent

SEEKING AND FINDING GOD

Faithful God,
you give us forty days of Lent to quiet ourselves
and explore the inner chambers of our hearts.
Let these sacred days be a time when we seek and find you there.
Passionate God,
may we find you even in our tears and in our pain
and in whatever troubles our hearts.
Keep us from all that separates us from you.
Be with us and in us.
Amen.

THE RISK

Holy God,
during this season of repentance we ponder the risk,
the greatest risk in all of human history.
This is the time to reflect on Jesus who risked all for us —
to show us His love and to show us how to love.
Let us be willing to stake our lives on our faith in you
because we know that your love for us is unconditional.
Make this Lenten season a time when we ponder our own risks
and muster the courage to take those that will promote your kingdom.

All loving God,
make us worthy of your outrageous love for us.
Make us worthy.
Amen.

RE-CREATION

God of mystery,
we journey with Jesus during this Lenten season
with the certain hope that you will re-create our world
so that all people will live in peace and justice.
Call us out of the wilderness of apathy
and help us to reach out to those who do not know hope or love.
Hear the longings of our hearts
and the cries of those who yearn to live in peace and justice.
Let Easter burst into a world waiting to be re-created.
Amen.

Holy Week

LEAD US OUT OF THE TOMB

God of life,
as we prepare to celebrate the Paschal Triduum
lead us out of all the tombs we have made for ourselves.
Lead us out of the tomb of complacency,
where we remain safe from involvement.
Lead us out of the tomb of despair,
where we have wallowed in our sorrow.
Lead us out of the tomb of pretense,
where we hide from the truth.
Lead us out of the tomb of indecision,
where we too easily avoid life's pain and spiritual growth.
Lead us out of the tomb of darkness,
where we hide from the light.
Lead us toward you,
who are our Light and our Life.
Lead us, loving God, to that eternal Easter Sunday,
when we will burst forth from our tombs
and fully experience your light and your Love.
Amen.

Easter

NEWNESS

The joy of Easter wells up inside of us
ready to erupt into a world in need of new life.
God of life,
the signs of Easter are real:
    water flowing freely,
    fire burning brightly,
    water, light, and life.
May we dance and sing for joy,
Rising out of the rubble
of all that keeps us in darkness.
Transform us, O God of mercy!
Pierce the darkness in our souls with your light.
Turn our sorrow into joy
and our grief into dancing.
Clean up all the messes of our lives.
God of all that is new,
form and re-form our lives this Easter.
Open our hearts to all that is new.
so that we can experience fully your power to renew our lives.
Pour your Easter energy into us.
Energize us with your light and free us with your love.
O God of eternal life,
move in us and well up inside of us,
course through us, breathing joy into our souls.
Let your Easter joy surround us, enfold us and make us new.
Amen.

PRAYERS FOR MEETINGS

RELYING ON GOD'S POWER IN US

Empowering God,
it is you who call us and guide us as we work.
It is your power in us that confirms our confidence and boosts our spirits.
Never let us act as though you are not a part of our plans.
We are confident that your Holy Spirit dwells in us and among us.
Help us to rely on the power of your Spirit
to inspire us to do our best work, giving you praise and glory through it.

Compared to your bountiful, limitless love for us
we have so little to offer you.
Bless our humble efforts and make them holy.

Lead us in the path of what is right and just
and may your peace, your goodness, and your deep caring
sustain us in all that we do.
Amen.

CONFIDENT OF GOD'S GUIDANCE

God of power, wisdom, and love,
we gather in your holy name
to do your work, confident of your constant guidance and inspiration.
We praise you and thank you for choosing us for this work.
We are people with limitations, and so rely on your eternal wisdom
to inspire us and to point us in the right direction.
Give us the gift of prudence
so that the decisions we make will only be those
that rise out of our intention to do your will
and to serve your people.
Amen.

WE ARE CHANNELS OF GOD'S ENERGY

Gracious God,
because we know of your love and mercy,
we gather as men and women of faith with a deep sense of commitment.
Give us passion for the tasks at hand.
Give us the grace to listen and respond to the prompting of your Spirit.
Let your energy be the driving force behind all that we say and do here.
Channel your energy and love through us
and let it flow through us to one another.
Bless our efforts here;
sustain us in the difficult moments.
Inspire us with your wisdom and comfort us with your love.
Be with us, Gracious God, as we attempt to do your work.
Amen.

CALLED AND CHOSEN

Holy God,
we gather in your name.
We come with one voice
to honor and praise you for choosing us as your people
and for calling us to be signs of your love in our world.

Help us to be men and women of vision.
Give us the daring to dream your dream.
Give us the faith and the fortitude we need
to help build a world bursting with promise.
Give us the wisdom and the determination
to act responsibly and compassionately.

Gracious God,
you are the great designer of all things.
Bless our plans and projects;
let our lives embody your truth.
and let your love flow through us.
Make us sources of your grace for those whom we lead;
make us a blessing from you to them.
Amen.

Doing God's Work

Empowering God,
you call us, you guide us, and you empower us to do your work.
Walk with us as we endeavor to make our plans a reality.
Light our way.
Keep us from stumbling in the dark.
Let us never forget that your blessing means everything to our work.

Do not allow anything we say or do
disrupt the flow of your blessing at this meeting.
Let our work always enhance, and never restrain, the work of your Spirit.

At the completion of our work,
give us a true sense of fulfillment,
and let us rest in the knowledge that we have served you well.
Amen.

A Blessing to Open a Meeting

Let us bow our heads and ask for God's blessing.

May God, who is the source of all blessings and all that is blessed,
be a part of this gathering
at its beginning and at its end
and during all the time in between.

May God's Holy Spirit guide us in all that is discerned and decided here.
May the Spirit inspire us with words that say all that they mean
yet fall gently on the ears of all gathered here.

May God bless us with the ability to speak with integrity
and to work with uncompromising diligence.

May God help us focus on what truly matters
and give us the insight to discern what is right.
May God fill our hearts with love
and may that love determine the course we take
and shape all our interactions.

May God give us
wisdom to make good decisions,

courage to take the necessary risks,
unshakable hope to maintain a steadfast Spirit,
good humor to keep things in perspective,
and deep trust so that as we risk, we remain grounded in God.

May God bless us with the personal joy of knowing
that we have acted out of love,
that we have done our best,
and that we have served God with all our hearts.
Amen.

PRAYERS TO CELEBRATE OUR HUMAN JOURNEY

FOR PERSONAL PEACE

Holy God, sentinel of my soul,
Rock my soul into calm and peace.
Amid the noise and the commotion of this fast-paced world,
attune my spirit to the quiet soothing whisper of your peace.

Quiet the pace of my busy days.
Slow down the beat of my heart.
Weave your peace deep within me.

Whisper your Word of peace into my heart.
Soak my soul with your love, so that no matter where I am,
I will rest in the security of your embrace.
Amen.

AWAKEN US

Loving Jesus,
awaken in us the passion that lies deep in our souls.
You have called us to live passionately;
to see greatness in small things
like mustard seeds and widow's mites;
to have wine-drenched celebrations
and treat one another with compassion.
Keep us from seeking grand things,
but give us moments of grand awareness so that we can see:
    your tenderness in a tiny baby,
    your power in a warm embrace,
    your passion in one another's eyes
    your joy in the laughter of children.

Jesus,
you were willing to risk all so that we would be free.
Give us the courage to risk what we are here and now
for what we can become.
Never allow us to give up the good fight,
for that is how we grow stronger and more faithful.
Give us moments of profound silence,
that we might hear your whisper deep in our hearts.
Whisper your word of life in us,
that we may awaken to your holy passion deep within us.
Amen.

WE RESONATE JESUS IN OUR LIVES

Jesus, Lord of life,
we approach you with our fears, hurts, and anxieties.
We come to you certain of your love for us
and yearning for your compassion
to soothe all that is aching
and unsettled
in our souls and in our world.

Jesus, you took two fish and five loaves and fed thousands.
Take our meager gifts and multiply them;
use them to satisfy the hungers of a famished, yearning world.

Jesus you chased the swindlers from the temple.
Help us to chase all that is dishonorable from our lives.

Jesus, you wrote in the sand and forgave a sinner.
Let us write your words of love on one another's hearts.

Jesus, you allowed the bleeding woman to touch you.
Let us touch you so that your love will flow through us to all people.

Jesus, you let the blind man see.
Help us see the pain in one another and become healers too.

Jesus, you loved Lazarus back to life.
Give us your life-giving love
and teach us to share it with those whose spirits have died.

Jesus, eternal lover,
let your life resonate in ours.
Make of us living signs of your invincible love.
Amen.

GIVE US WHAT WE NEED

Gracious God,
you are the great giver of gifts.
We come today with arms outstretched,
asking you to give us what we need to live our lives fully.

Give us courage
to face our inner demons and chase them away.
Give us wisdom
to name our gifts and use them for the good of all.
Give us strength
to change even those things which we have held most dearly.
Give us the gift of remembering
who we are and to whom we belong.
Give us the gift of single-heartedness
to focus on your call in our lives.
Give us a visible faith
so that through us others can believe.
Give us steadfast love
to melt away the walls that separate us.
Give us a deep sense of your presence in our lives.
For with you we have it all,
all we need to be in love with life,
to be whole and happy and fulfilled.
Amen.

AN OFFERING

Tender God, Breath of Life,
before we were born you imprinted your Spirit on our souls,
and poured your love into our hearts.
Through years of growing pains and losses,
triumphs and troubles,
you have sustained us with your love.
Today we offer back to you the stories of our lives.

We offer you all the dreams we have dared to dream;
and our yearnings deep inside;
the tears that have gushed in our souls,
and filled our eyes to overflowing.
We offer you the compromises that have diminished us
and those that have made us strong.
Accept anew all our fears and doubts, our guilt and regrets.
Accept all the risks we have taken and those we were too afraid to take;
We give you all our losses and the empty places they have left inside us.

We offer you all those whose hearts are melded to ours:
those who have loved us
and those whose words of affirmation are imprinted on our hearts.
We offer you those who challenge us to risk and grow;
who recognize our gifts and enable us to use them,
urging us to be all that we can be.
We offer you those who try us with their words and deeds;
and those who have broken our hearts.

We put before you, loving God,
    all that we are,
    all that we have ever done;
    and owned,
    and loved.
Take our stories and make them holy,
imperfect offerings to you
in thanksgiving for the gift of life.
Amen.

PRAYER TO THE GOD OF ALL CONSOLATION

Jesus,
when you met the sinful woman, you traced compassion in the sand.
Today when we come seeking your compassion,
trace words of consolation for us upon the sands of time.
Take us from all that crushes our spirits.
Mend our broken hearts and heal the scars of our youth.

God of All Consolation,
When the world shatters around us,
piece it together with your tender care.
When deep-grown fear haunts us,
whisper a word of peace to us.
When the darkness seems to swallow us,
lead us toward your light.
When all seems lost,
bring us back to the comfort of your compassion.
Amen.

PRAYER TO A LAUGHING GOD

Compassionate God,
you broke into a world heavy with sorrow and profound injustice.
You sent us Jesus who told us not to be afraid;
who said that nothing would harm us, not even death.
Through Jesus you showed us that you are a laughing God;
a God of joy that overcomes sorrow;
a God of life that conquers death.

God of laughter,
have a laugh on us.
Laugh in us and with us.
Help us to laugh our frivolous worries away.
Give each of us the gift of humor,
for it lends perspective to all that seems dark and dreadful.
Let our humor remind us that we are a people of hope.

God of Joy,
May we always encounter people who are willing to walk in the rain,
to play and to laugh out loud — loudly.
Put people in our path who are willing
to risk looking foolish for love,
to wait at the end of the line,
to stand while others sit and rest.

Send us people who are willing
to hear the music over the deafening noises of a troubled world
and to play it when burdens weigh us down.
Give us people who are willing
to cry when life hurts and when it feels good,
to dream outrageous dreams and die a little each day.

Help us to not take ourselves too seriously.
Let our laughter remind us that we are a people redeemed,
who believe in a better tomorrow.
Remind us that we are people of a laughing God,
who know that the best is yet to come.
God of laughter,
have a laugh on us.
Laugh in us.
Laugh with us.
Amen.

IN THANKSGIVING FOR THE PEOPLE WHO BLESS OUR LIVES

All-loving and passionate God,
in your creative genius you filled the earth with human beings.
We are creatures in search of others like ourselves.
Today we come in thanksgiving
for the special people who bless our lives.

Thank you for all those whom we love
and for those who give love in return.

Thank you for our personal advocates:
for those who believe in us, urging us to be more.
for those who comfort us when we fail,
then help us to re-focus and re-create.
Thank you for those who are always there for us
through the trials and the celebrations.
Thank you for those who cry with us
and shout and cheer and sing for joy with us.

Thank you for the healers in our lives:
for those who hold us
and those who offer words that soothe;
for those who forgive before we ask and who free us to be ourselves.

Thank you for those whose lives make our lives holy:
for those whose commitment to justice inspires us;
whose integrity fills us with awe;
and those whose holiness draws us closer to you.

Thank you for our personal prophets:
those who disturb our complacency
and those who call us away from our self-serving;
and speak the bittersweet truth to us.
We thank you for those who don't offer the easy answers
but stand by us in the questioning.
We thank you for those who confront our demons with us.

Thank you for those who stretch us to be more:
for those who trust us, care for us, and empower us,
for those who see through us and still love us;

for those who stir our souls to seek and find and live
the truth about ourselves.
Thank you for those whose eyes penetrate our souls
and speak love to us without a word.

God of love,
thank you for friends and lovers,
for confidants and prophets,
for soulmates and advocates.
Thank you for those who are
living, breathing signs of your freeing love for us.
Amen.

RESHAPING A MISSHAPEN WORLD

God of peace,
your call is clear.
We are to reshape a misshapen world.
Bless us with your peace
so that through our actions
we may change the course of human history.
Give us the grace to never dishonor ourselves
with prejudice, apathy, or hatred.
Let us stand firm against anything that is dehumanizing.
Guard us against indifference and complacency.
Ignite our hearts with your love and your justice,
so that our commitment of conscience will stand out
like the brightest light in the darkest night.

Loving God,
we are your imperfect people, yet we trust in your love for us.
Turn our complacency into commitment
to ease the pain of those who suffer.
Turn our bitterness into renewed purpose to stop injustice.
Turn our apathy into resolve to put an end to oppression.
Turn our indifference into new energy to serve those in need.
Turn our stubbornness into determination to bring peace to all humanity.

Empowering God,
Give power to the powerless
and strength to the weak.
Give joy to those who despair
and freedom to those who have been robbed of it.
Give satisfaction to those who hunger
for bread and for justice.

God of all,
let new life rise out of the ashes of human suffering.
May generations to come be architects of peace and justice.
May they be full of strength and courage
and passionate about bringing your love to all humanity.
Amen